SLAM!™
STARS OF WRESTLING

TRIPLE H

NO MERCY

BRIDGET HEOS

rosen publishing's
rosen
central®

New York

For Brent and Cooper, wrestling guys

Published in 2012 by The Rosen Publishing Group, Inc.
29 East 21st Street, New York, NY 10010

First Edition

Library of Congress Cataloging-in-Publication Data

Heos, Bridget.
Triple H: no mercy/Bridget Heos.
    p. cm.—(Slam! stars of wrestling)
Includes bibliographical references and index.
ISBN 978-1-4488-5539-1 (library binding)—ISBN 978-1-4488-5603-9 (pbk.)—
ISBN 978-1-4488-5604-6 (6-pack)
1. Triple H, 1969—Juvenile literature.
2. Wrestlers—United States—Biography—Juvenile literature. I. Title.
GV1196.T75H46 2012
796.812092—dc23
[B]

2011022750

Manufactured in the United States of America

CPSIA Compliance Information: Batch #W12YA: For further information, contact Rosen Publishing, New York, New York, at 1-800-237-9932.

CONTENTS

INTRODUCTION

Triple H's tag team partner, Stone Cold Steve Austin, was in trouble. Chris Jericho had him locked in a finishing move called the Walls of Jericho. Jericho held Austin's legs behind him like he was a wheelbarrow. If Jericho pinned Austin, the match would be over. The rules in a tag team match say that one wrestler must stand on the apron (just outside the ropes) and wait to be tagged. Austin was nowhere near his teammate Triple H. Luckily for them, in professional wrestling, the rules are more like guidelines.

Unable to stand watching his teammate suffer any longer, Triple H stormed the ring and tackled Jericho. Austin was free of his grip. But something was wrong. Triple H rolled slowly out of the ring to battle Jericho on the ground. Now he was limping on one leg. Was it all part of the plan, or was Triple H really hurt? In pro wrestling, the matches are scripted, meaning the wrestlers plan out their moves ahead of time, and the outcome is predetermined. They don't try to hurt each other, but wrestlers often get hurt.

Now, still favoring his right leg, Triple H removed the cover from the announcer's table. As he wrestled Jericho onto the table, the two were head to head. Unbeknownst to the crowd, Jericho asked Triple H if he was OK. Triple H said that he thought he had torn his quadriceps, (the muscle above the kneecap). Jericho asked Triple H what he wanted to do. To Jericho's surprise, his opponent said he wanted to end the match as planned.

Triple H celebrates defeating Randy Orton at WrestleMania XXV on April 5, 2009. The victory allowed Triple H to keep the coveted WWE championship belt.

That meant undergoing the Walls of Jericho, a maneuver that strains the quadriceps.

Once on the table, Jericho grabbed Triple H's legs, flipped him onto his stomach, and held him in the Walls of Jericho. However, the wrestlers inside the ring determine the outcome of the match. Austin was still fighting with Jericho's teammate, Chris Benoit. Austin had temporarily knocked out Benoit. Jericho now stormed the ring to battle Austin.

Jericho had nearly pinned Austin when Triple H limped into the ring. He tried to attack Jericho but missed and hit Austin's arm instead. Benoit rose from the mat to wrestle Triple H onto the floor while Jericho pinned Austin. Austin writhed in the agony of defeat. Meanwhile, Triple H lay curled up on the floor, facing the ring. Nobody could see his face or see how much pain he was in. He had wrestled through a torn quadriceps, possibly making the injury even worse. Now he couldn't walk. Off camera, two WWE officials arrived to help him out of the arena. He leaned on them, trying to bear the pain.

1 A VERY YOUNG BODYBUILDER

Born in 1969 in Nashua, New Hampshire, Paul Michael Levesque grew up playing baseball and basketball. His favorite sport to watch on television was pro wrestling. In fact, to this day, it is the only sport he watches. Paul's favorite wrestler was Ric Flair, even though his father hated the bad guy wrestler, or heel. Flair's routine was to whip the crowd up into a hateful frenzy. They wanted him to lose so badly! Then Flair would lose. Paul's father thought Flair must be a bad wrestler because he usually lost. But even at an early age, Paul knew that Flair was a good wrestler because he entertained the crowd.

To Paul, muscular athletes such as wrestlers were larger than life. One day, when he was fourteen years old, he and a friend drove past a new gym called Muscles in Motion. They went in and were given a free weeklong membership. Inside, there were lots of bodybuilders. Paul wanted to be part of that. He had his own money from a paper route, so his parents, Paul and Patricia, told him that he could join the gym.

Paul not only joined, but also immersed himself in the whole lifestyle. He changed his diet, eating healthy foods like chicken breasts and pasta. Eventually, he even stopped hanging out with his high school classmates. The guys at the gym were now his friends. They would encourage each other, whether trying to meet a personal best at the gym or participating in a weightlifting competition outside the gym. Paul was only a teen but matched the guys set for set (although he couldn't lift as much weight). Even when he could barely move

Ric Flair, shown here in 1985 wrestling Chief Wahoo McDaniel, was one of Paul Levesque's favorite pro wrestlers. Paul, now known as Triple H, later worked with Flair.

following a grueling workout, he returned to the gym the next day. The guys saw in him an unusual drive. They accepted him as one of the big guys.

At age seventeen, Paul was 6 foot 4 (2 meters), 210 pounds (95 kilograms). Coaches wanted him to join the football and wrestling teams, but his heart was set on becoming a pro wrestler. He subscribed to every wrestling magazine and watched the WWF (which today is the WWE). Paul also started competing in bodybuilding events, competitions in which people are judged for their muscular appearances. He won Teen Mr. New Hampshire at age nineteen. But his dream wasn't to become a professional bodybuilder. He still wanted to wrestle for the WWF. To do that, he needed to enroll in wrestling school. But he didn't know how to find one. Unlike today, wrestling schools didn't promote themselves. There were no Web sites (or even the Internet). Back then, you had to know somebody who knew somebody.

Finally, that person came into Paul's life. Ted Arcidi was well-known in the sport of powerlifting. In 1985, he had set the bench press record at 705 pounds (320 kg). To make extra money, he had joined the pro wrestling circuit. He hated it. Arcidi began working out at Paul's gym. But when Paul asked him about pro wrestling, the powerlifter tried to discourage the young bodybuilder. He said it was an incredibly tough business.

For Paul, learning that wrestling was a tough business wasn't discouraging at all. He was so obsessed with the sport that he was willing to do whatever it took to break into it—and succeed at it. He just needed to know where the closest wrestling school was. Finally, Arcidi told him about Walter "Killer" Kowalski's school in Malden, Massachusetts.

Upon graduating from high school in 1987, Paul had gone to work as a manager at Gold's Gym. (Sadly for him and his friends, Muscles in Motion had closed down.) Kowalski's school was an hour commute from the Nashua gym. He could keep his job while pursuing his dream.

Lifting weights has been part of Triple H's workouts since he was fourteen. He competed in body-building competitions but always knew he wanted to be a wrestler.

School of Wrestling

Over the phone, Killer Kowalski, a former pro wrestling heel, also tried to discourage Paul. Kowalski wanted Paul to know that his school offered no guarantee of success in the cut-throat business of wrestling. Paul just wanted to know when he could start.

In his autobiography and workout guide, *Making the Game: Triple H's Approach to a Better Body*, Triple H describes what happened when he finally met Kowalski in person. The teacher said, "You're a big one, ain't ya?" When he said it, Paul sensed that someone believed in him. Of course, Kowalski first had to see whether Paul showed talent in the ring.,

The gym itself seemed designed to discourage aspiring wrestlers. The nearly concrete floor of the boxing—not wrestling—ring was unforgiving. When Paul arrived, the other guys were doing a move called the "Hard Way In," where they stood on the apron and flipped themselves over the rope. They were to land inside the ring—flat on their backs. Paul had

When Triple H met Walter "Killer" Kowalski, he was running a wrestling school. But he had been one of wrestling's biggest heels. Here, he flies onto Buddy Rogers on October 24, 1962.

BODYBUILDING, WEIGHTLIFTING, AND POWERLIFTING

Bodybuilding is a competition in which contestants are judged for their muscular builds. Athletes achieve the high muscle build and definition through weightlifting and diet. Some have also admitted to using steroids as part of their training.

Weightlifting is an Olympic sport in which competitors lift a barbell over their heads, either in a clean and jerk move or snatch move. The athlete who lifts the most weight wins.

Powerlifting is a competitive sport—featured in the World Games but not the Olympics—in which athletes participate in three events: squat, bench press, and dead lift. As in Olympic weightlifting, they are competing to see who can lift the most weight.

never been in a wrestling ring, but while the other guys struggled with the move, Paul got it the first time.

Many young students realized during their first day at Killer Kowalski's school that the sport wasn't for them. The opposite was true for Paul. He felt an instant connection to wrestling.

Kowalski's first impression of Paul's potential never waned. He took the young rookie under his wing. He told him he had the look, build, and charisma to be a star. But Paul wasn't so easily swayed. He hadn't taken Arcidi's discouraging words to heart. Now he didn't let Kowalski's words of encouragement go to his head. He knew that it really would be tough to make it in the business. He also knew that he would never be satisfied with just being a wrestler. He would want top billing, like Ric Flair. He gave himself three years to make it. If wrestling didn't pan out, he would focus on the gym business—perhaps owning some of his own gyms.

Patricia, Paul's mother, was even more skeptical of wrestling. She thought it was an inherently unstable job. Paul's father, on the other hand, saw no harm in giving it a try. After all, Paul was working his way up the ranks faster than most wrestlers. Three months into training, Kowalski had Paul performing in the school's independent circuit, the International Wrestling Federation (IWF). Kowalski wanted Paul to wrestle under the name the Terrorizer. Paul changed the name to Terra Ryzing.

Terra Ryzing's debut was in Burlington, Vermont. It was a small gig with little compensation. While Paul was promised $50, he was only paid $25. But his discouraging financial situation was overshadowed by signs of a bright future. Kowalski told Paul he was going to win the title. Also, a top WWF talent scout, Pat Patterson, pulled Paul aside one night and told him he had potential. He should stick with it.

Paul knew it was time to join a bigger promotion to prepare himself for the WWF. He had professional photos taken and put together a highlights tape and résumé. On the résumé, he claimed he'd been wrestling for five years, when really he'd been wrestling for only one.

2 THE ROAD TO THE WWF VIA WCW

It was 1994, and Paul Levesque was twenty-five years old. If he wanted to advance his wrestling career, he needed to make his move. Living in Nashua, he had to network creatively. He learned that his Gold's Gym used the same consulting firm as Ric Flair's gym. Members of the firm told him about a seminar where Flair would be speaking. At the time, Flair was working for World Championship Wrestling (WCW,) the WWF's top competitor.

Levesque went to the seminar, bringing his tape and résumé in case he met Flair. He did, briefly, but didn't get a chance to pass on the materials. However, he also met Chip Burnham, a promoter and ticket salesman for WCW. He and Chip spent the evening talking about the wrestling business. Afterward, Burnham asked him for his résumé and tape. He would pass it on to his friend Bob Due, the president of WCW.

Just a few weeks later, he got a call at Gold's Gym. Due said he was passing the tape and résumé on to Eric Bischoff, a new executive at WCW. However, the conversation with Bischoff didn't go so smoothly. Bischoff didn't want to pay for him to visit Atlanta for a tryout. Levesque said that he would pay his own way, and Bischoff finally agreed.

In the locker room before the match, Levesque faced the typical rookie welcome: nobody talked to him. Well, one wrestler was friendly: Arn Anderson, an original member of Flair's stable (or group of wrestlers), the Four Horsemen. That was a good sign. After the match, he received further reassurance that his trip to Atlanta had been worth it. The guys in the locker room said he'd done a good job.

He was hired by WCW and signed a one-year, $50,000 contract. He traveled with the WCW roster and got to know the veteran wrestlers. That's when his padded résumé caught up with him. Rookie wrestlers tend to botch moves—either making them look unrealistic or, worse, causing injury. To the longtime wrestlers of WCW, Levesque's inexperience showed. A wrestler named Terry Taylor asked him if he had really wrestled for five years. Levesque was straight with Taylor. He said that, in truth, he had wrestled for only one year.

Taylor offered to teach him at the WCW training facility, the Power Plant. He jumped at the chance. Taylor and the trainer at Power Plant, Jody Hamilton, helped him to polish his wrestling moves. Taylor also became a friend. Levesque, who was still known as Terra Ryzing, was improving. Even his childhood hero Flair took note. He told Levesque he should keep working with Taylor.

One day, Flair, who worked in the creative offices of WCW, called him to CNN Center to

After a rocky start over the phone, Eric Bischoff hired Triple H to join WCW. But with little experience, Triple H would rely on training from veterans of the sport.

Triple H has gone through a variety of looks over the years. Here, he is clean-shaven and wearing long dreadlocks as former heavyweight champion Mike Tyson threatens to punch him at WrestleMania XIV.

help shoot some promos. Levesque had no idea that the promos were for him, but it was certainly good news. Promos air on television or on the big screen during wrestling events. As the name implies, they promote a particular wrestler. They are meant to get fans excited about a new or returning character.

But he was caught off guard by the character they would be introducing. He would now be known as Jean-Paul Levesque, a French guy. Flair asked him if he spoke French. He said he didn't. Flair said that he would at least have to speak with a French accent. And one more thing: he was now a bad guy. This odd turn of events would work in Levesque's favor, but at the time, he found the whole thing odd.

As Jean-Paul Levesque, he began tag team wrestling with Lord Steven Regal, a British aristocrat. They were known as the Bluebloods. They hit it off great— in and out of the ring. But Levesque's contract was running out. His goal was still to work for the WWF. He called the promotion to see if it was interested in him. Both Bischoff and Vince McMahon, the owner of the WWF, made offers. The WWF offered an unspecified amount and would require him to work three hundred days a year. The WCW offered him a two-day-a-week job and set pay. The decision seemed easy. And it was. But not in the way Bischoff expected. Levesque left for the WWF. He wanted to work more hours. He thought it would make him a better wrestler.

It was hard to leave guys like Taylor, who had shown him the ropes. It was hard to part ways with Flair, who had been his inspiration all along. He felt better about his decision when Flair stopped him on his way out. According to *Making the Game*, Flair said, "You go wrestle for him like you're capable, and Vince McMahon will make you a star."

Hunter Hearst Helmsley

In 1995, Levesque had his first meeting with McMahon. The WWF owner said that he liked his snobbish persona. However, McMahon thought it would be easier for him to turn baby face (good guy) someday if his character was from America. McMahon himself lived in a nice neighborhood in Connecticut. The new persona he created for Levesque was Hunter Hearst Helmsley, the Connecticut Blueblood.

He was surprised by how much effort went into the creation of Hunter Hearst Helmsley. Unlike at WCW, McMahon didn't simply call him into his office and say, "You're from Connecticut now." Instead, the WWF creative team and marketing team got involved. They sought his input and offered advice. Levesque wanted to look perfect in his new role as an American aristocrat. In order to lose body fat and never appear winded, he added more cardiovascular training to his workout. (Cardiovascular exercises raise your heart rate and burn calories.)

On the April 30, 1995, episode of *WWF Wrestling Challenge*, Hunter Hearst Helmsley—or Triple H—was introduced to fans everywhere. Triple H quickly began a feud with Marc Mero, the Wildman, and his girlfriend, Sable. In true heel fashion, Triple H tricked Mero into putting his Intercontinental Championship belt on the line. Triple H challenged Curt Hennig, Mr. Perfect, to a match, and then injured him backstage. Mero took

WCW VS. THE WWF: RIVAL WRESTLING GIANTS

The WWF (World Wrestling Federation) was an offshoot of Capitol Wrestling Corporation (CWC), which was run by Vince McMahon's father. In 1982, McMahon purchased CWC and renamed it WWF. He expanded the promotion beyond its original region. He televised shows across the nation and recruited talent from other regional promotions. Soon, many of the regional promotions folded. The WWF became more and more powerful. Following McMahon's vision, it also appealed to a wider audience. Stars like Hulk Hogan and Andre the Giant became household names.

In the early 1990s, World Championship Wrestling (WCW) began competing with the WWF for domination of Monday night television. WCW had evolved from the National Wrestling Association, which was the regional pro wrestling system that had persisted for years. Now it was a national promotion owned by billionaire Ted Turner.

The two companies vied for top talent. WCW became known as the promotion with veteran stars, whereas the WWF was the promotion where new talent could shine. Eventually, the WWF purchased WCW. The WWF was renamed WWE.

Andre the Giant battles Sergeant Slaughter in 1981, when pro wrestling was gaining a wider audience. Andre the Giant and other wrestlers would soon become household names.

Hennig's place, and Triple H won the belt. It was the first of many heel victories for Triple H.

The following year, a match brought to light the serious injuries that can occur in pro wrestling. Though scripted, the sport can hardly be called fake. When wrestlers are seen landing on their backs or knees or head, that's really happening. While the impact is at times exaggerated, it can still have serious consequences.

On May 28, 1996, Triple H went against Marty Garner on *WWF Superstars*. Triple H attempted his signature move, the Pedigree. In this move, he lifts the opponent off his feet, flips him, and lands him on his face. This is supposed to be done softly, to reduce the risk of head injury. But Garner mistook the move for one in which he would need to jump to gain momentum. Rather than letting himself be lifted, Garner jumped, resulting in him landing hard on his head. He suffered a neck injury but luckily was not paralyzed.

Triple H himself would be no stranger to injuries during the course of his career. But for now, things were going well for him. Backstage, he became known as a member of the Clique (also spelled "Kliq"). This was a group of wrestlers who influenced McMahon and the creative team. Others in the Clique were Shawn Michaels, Kevin Nash, Sean Waltman, and Scott Hall. The group was obsessed with wrestling and came up with many storylines, some adopted by McMahon. Triple H says that McMahon also had a meeting with members of the Clique in which he gave them the roster and asked who they would want on their team if they owned the WWF. That suggests a certain amount of power wielded by the Clique.

Overall, the Clique wanted the WWF to move toward more reality-based characters, as opposed to over-the-top gimmicks. Ironically, Triple H found himself participating in a gimmick that was truly over-the-top. He got into a feud with Henry Godwinn, a farmer-wrestler whose finishing move was to throw pig slop on his opponent. Some guys wouldn't let Godwinn do this because they didn't want to be laughed at. But Triple H thought the fans would love it. Night after night, he got pig slop thrown on him. This proved to McMahon that Triple H was willing to do what Ric Flair had always done—entertain the crowd, even if it made him look bad.

Triple H's star was rising. He was scheduled to win King of the Ring in 1996 and then enter a feud with fellow Clique member—and the most popular wrestler at the time—Shawn Michaels. However, none of this ended up happening. Triple H was about to get in big trouble from the boss.

3 FROM THE CLIQUE TO D-GENERATION X

When Triple H left WCW, he'd joined its biggest rival, the WWF. On September 4, 1995, WCW first aired *Monday Night Nitro* to challenge the WWF's *Monday Night Raw*. This television rivalry, which lasted until 2001, was called the "Monday Night Wars." Both companies wanted the best ratings—that is, the most television viewers. To achieve this, they vied for the top talent, both in the ring and behind the scenes.

On May 19, 1996, Scott Hall and Kevin Nash were leaving the WWF to join WCW as New World Order, or nWo. It was a big coup for WCW, who planned to give fans a glimpse of the politics occurring backstage between the WWF and WCW. (With the dawn of the Internet, fans were discussing insider rumors online concerning the two rival companies.) To the WWF, Hall and Nash were popular wrestlers. To Triple H and Shawn Michaels, they were good friends and part of the Clique.

The night of their departure, Triple H wrestled Hall, and Michaels wrestled Nash. Michaels pinned Nash but then kissed him on the cheek. Nash "woke up" and the two hugged farewell. Hall and Triple H also joined them on the stage, and the four hugged. The crowd was cheering, apparently happy that the backstage friendship between Hall, Nash, Michaels, and Triple H was being acknowledged. But people in the office—and some wrestlers— thought it broke with tradition. They thought a wrestler should never break character during the show.

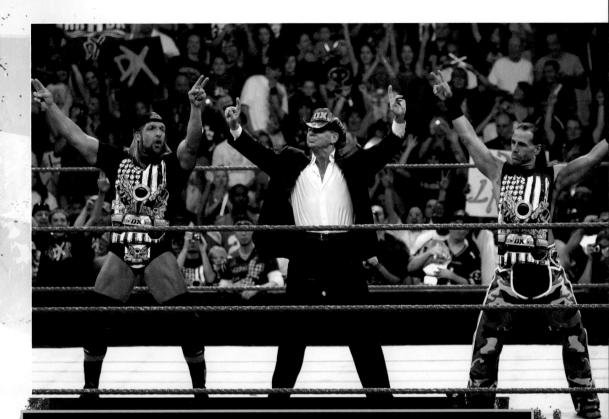

Triple H and Shawn Michaels formed D-Generation X in 1997, along with Chyna and Ravishing Rick Rude. The team was revived many times, including on *Raw* on August 24, 2009, shown here.

McMahon felt compelled to punish someone for the transgression. Nash and Hall were out of reach; they were moving to WCW. Michaels was too big of a draw to suspend; it would result in a loss in ratings. Triple H was a wrestler who showed promise but didn't yet have a loyal fan base. McMahon told Triple H that he was going to take the fall. McMahon even offered the wrestler a chance to get out of his contract and return to WCW. If he

Instead of Triple H, Stone Cold Steve Austin won King of the Ring in 1996. He became a hugely popular star, known for challenging authority. Here, he competes at WrestleMania XVIII in 2002.

remained with the WWF, he would not win King of the Ring as scheduled or begin a program with Michaels.

Triple H didn't want to return to WCW. But he asked McMahon to promise him something: in six months, the punishment would end. He didn't want to stay with the WWF if the grudge was going to last forever. McMahon agreed. While Triple H temporarily became what is known as a jobber—someone who routinely loses to advance others' careers—Stone Cold Steve Austin won King of the Ring. He became a hugely popular star—a hero for working-class America.

However, true to his word, six months later, McMahon allowed Triple H to rise again. In 1997, Triple H and Shawn Michaels formed D-Generation X. Triple H brought on Chyna, a female bodybuilder and wrestler, as his bodyguard. Hunter Hearst Helmsley officially shortened his name to Triple H and dropped the blueblood persona. Now, he wore T-shirts and leather.

Ravishing Rick Rude was also a part of the new stable. D-Generation X wrestlers were irreverent members of the so-called slacker generation. One of their most infamous acts involved Bret Hart's final night with the WWF. Hart, a Canadian and the WWF champion, was leaving for WCW. His final match was in Montreal on November 9, 1997. Hart asked McMahon to let his last match against Shawn Michaels end in a disqualification rather than a pin. McMahon agreed but behind Hart's back asked the referee to blow the whistle early. Hart was pinned. Hart—and his Canadian fans—were furious. And it wasn't just an act. They truly felt betrayed.

Within the WWF, other wrestlers were angry, too. They felt like they could no longer trust their boss, McMahon. But, on stage at least, DX, as D-Generation X was sometimes known, was undaunted. The next night, Triple H, Michaels, and Chyna came swaggering onto the stage, bragging about the victory and insulting the heartbroken Canadian audience. They were clearly heels.

TRIPLE H'S DIET AND EXERCISE

Triple H tries to eat six small, healthy meals a day. Breakfast may be a bagel, protein shake, and piece of fruit, for instance. Because he is often on the road, he relies on fast food and convenience stores. He orders the healthiest option on the menu. At a gas station, he'll buy milk or yogurt instead of soda or candy.

Triple H gained his incredible strength through weightlifting, and as a wrestler, he continued to lift weights. While wrestling full time, he relied on ring time as his cardiovascular training. He also scaled back on weightlifting so that he wouldn't wear out his body. Still, he hit the gym four days a week, focusing on a different body region each time: shoulders and triceps, chest and biceps, legs, and back and rear.

But, in America at least, they were popular heels, meaning they had the potential to turn face. Their crude antics started being copied elsewhere in pop culture. For instance, football players, after scoring a touchdown, would imitate the karate chop–like gestures that DX did on stage. Soon the group faced a crisis, though. Michaels had an injured back. At WrestleMania XIV, he lost the title to Austin. Now he needed to take a break from wrestling.

Triple H Leads His Generation

Instead of letting DX fall apart, Triple H became the leader, claiming Michaels had dropped the ball. (In real life, Triple H knew that Michaels was out due to injury, and the two remained friends.) As the head of DX, Triple H's biggest stunt was to raid WCW, which was performing at a nearby venue. Triple H and his crew arrived at WCW in a Jeep fashioned to look like a tank. Though officials wouldn't let them inside, they told jokes and made fun of WCW outside the building. The WCW fans thought it was funny, and word spread of their prank. DX became fan favorites and turned face. Triple H believed his strength lay in being a heel. So he turned against DX.

Often, the WWF prefers to have a good guy hold the championship title. After all, the WWF champion is the face of the company, and most fans prefer good guys. Now, the WWF was going to allow Triple H, a heel, to become champion. He was to defeat Stone Cold Steve Austin. So that Austin didn't have to lose his belt to a non–title holder, the match was a triple threat with Mankind. Mankind won. The following night, on August 23, 1999, Triple H beat Mankind for the title belt. He was named WWF World Champion.

He wouldn't hold the title for long. On September 16, 1999, on Smack-Down, he lost it to the boss himself, Vince McMahon (who sometimes wrestled). A new angle developed in which McMahon was the good guy owner who hated that a bad guy was the champion. They incorporated a second storyline into this rivalry. A writer for the show had created a story in which Vince's daughter, Stephanie McMahon, was going to marry a wrestler named Test. When the writer left for WCW, nobody knew how the story was supposed to end.

In real life, Triple H convinced McMahon to write him into the story. On the show, he would trick Stephanie into marrying him. Stephanie was supposed to be the victim of Triple H's evil plan. But the crowd turned on her. So the writers let her turn heel. Now, it was Triple H and her against Vince. When they defeated him together, Vince left the business (according to the story). Triple H and Stephanie took over the WWF, ushering in the McMahon-Helmsley Era (again, fictionally). Fans hated the new "owners." In wrestling, that's a good thing. Not only were they wrestling's biggest

In 1999, the World Championship title was determined by triple threat. First, Mankind (*left*) battled Steve Austin. Mankind won. Triple H defeated Mankind for the belt.

power couple, but in real life, Triple H and Stephanie were beginning to like each other.

In 2000, Triple H took on a new nickname: the Game. As top heel, he went up against top faces like the Rock. They endured a sixty-minute Iron Man match and battled for the Intercontinental Championship in a ladder match at SummerSlam. The following year, in an odd twist, Triple H's long-time rival Steve Austin became his tag team partner. Though they made a powerful pair, the match would turn out to be among the most painful of Triple H's career.

The team went up against Chris Jericho and Chris Benoit. While running to rescue Austin from Jericho's signature move, the Walls of Jericho, Triple H felt his left quadriceps tear away from the bone. Though in excruciating pain, he finished the match.

When the match ended, he was rushed to the hospital. Initially, the doctor, Jim Andrews, guessed that Triple H had torn his quadriceps and that it would take six months to recover. But during surgery, Andrews saw that the tear was much worse than he had thought. He told Triple H it would take a year to recover. In reality, Andrews and his colleagues knew of no professional athletes who had come back from this injury. The doctor thought Triple H's wrestling career was over.

4 THE RETURN OF THE GAME

After his quadriceps surgery, Triple H was in a wheelchair. He set small goals for himself, like being able to walk with crutches. He moved to Birmingham, Alabama, to work with a physical therapist. By now, Triple H and Stephanie McMahon were dating. Stephanie, who was a WWF executive, would bring her work to the rehab center so that she could be with Triple H.

Triple H would rehab from 9 AM to 6 PM and then go to the gym until 9 PM. His primary goal—beyond walking—was to improve his range of motion (the extent to which his leg could move and bend). The process was painful, but he wanted to improve each day. The physical therapists would sometimes tell him he had reached his goal—even if he hadn't—just so that he would leave at night. They knew that healing would take longer than Triple H hoped.

Triple H wouldn't be content with healing alone. He also wanted to return to wrestling. Vince McMahon sent a wrestling ring to Birmingham, which was installed across the street from the rehab center. The physical therapist would watch Triple H's movements in the ring to see which leg muscles needed to be strengthened through physical therapy.

After months of hard work, Triple H was scheduled to return to the WWF on January 7, 2002, at Madison Square Garden. His return was heavily promoted. Still, he worried that when he walked out, the fans wouldn't care. But when Triple H walked onto stage, the roar of the crowd was deafening.

He was moved but waited until he was backstage to cry. He says in his autobiography, "If…everything I had gone through with my leg was just

Stephanie McMahon and Triple H, shown here in 2002 at WrestleMania XXVIII, were hated heels. In real life, however, they were dating.

for that one moment, that one moment when I walked through that curtain and heard that crowd and it all shut off right there, it would have all been worth it." However, Triple H had many years of his career ahead of him, starting with winning the championship at WrestleMania 18 (or X8.)

Meanwhile, changes were occurring in pro wrestling. Triple H's former employer, WCW was purchased by the WWF. The WWF was sued by the World Wide Fund for Nature over use of the WWF initials. The wrestling promotion changed its name to WWE. Big changes were happening in Triple H's life, too. He married Stephanie McMahon on October 25, 2003.

That year, Triple H also became good friends with Ric Flair, who had joined WWE when WCW was purchased. Triple H wanted to help Flair build his confidence as a wrestler, which had been shaken while at WCW. On stage, Triple H formed a new stable with Flair, Randy Orton, and Batista. They were called Evolution. At Armageddon, all the members of Evolution brought home a title.

The next year, a feud would pit Triple H against the McMahon family. Triple H had reunited with Shawn Michaels to reform D-Generation X. In real life, Triple H and Stephanie were welcoming their first daughter, Aurora Rose, into